5-8

D0607472

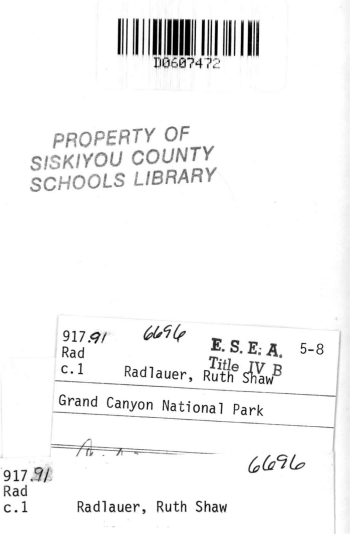

GRAND CANYON
National Park

by Ruth Radlauer

Design and photographs
by Rolf Zillmer

AN ELK GROVE BOOK

CHILDRENS PRESS, CHICAGO

The author is indebted to all Grand Canyon National Park personnel. In particular, she thanks Park Ranger Bill Clark and John C. O'Brien, Chief, Division of Interpretation, for their patient assistance in condensing two billion years into two pages.

The illustrator extends his gratitude to park personnel who helped with photography.

With special thanks to John Melvin, spinner of tales about Dan Canyon.

Photo top of page 21 by Ed Radlauer

Cover Photo: Grand Canyon, South Rim

Library of Congress Cataloging in Publication Data

Radlauer, Ruth Shaw.
    Grand Canyon National Park.
    (Parks for people)
    "An Elk Grove book."
    SUMMARY: Introduces the many enjoyments to be found in Grand Canyon National Park.
    1. Grand Canyon National Park—Juvenile literature. [1. Grand Canyon National Park. 2. National parks and reserves] I. Zillmer, Rolf. II. Title.
    F788.R33   917.91'32'045   76-58525
    ISBN 0-516-07492-X

Contents

What is Grand Canyon National Park?

Grand Canyon National Park is a story that started two billion years ago. When you hear this story, you begin to sense how old the earth is.

Only by looking into the canyon can you know its size. Standing alone on a point, you feel like a tiny dot in space, like a wink in time.

For you, Grand Canyon may be a picture story of a sunrise seen from a quiet place like Yavapai or Yaki Point. It may be the story of a canyon treefrog or a lizard on the trail.

Grand Canyon is easy walks or long, hard hiking down to the Colorado River. It may be a mule ride into the canyon or a float trip down the river.

This park is color. The rich reds and brown change from minute to minute, from morning to night, and from day to day.

Grand Canyon is sound. It's the hoarse caw of the raven and the rustle of wind in the juniper trees. Deep in the canyon it's the rushing roar of the Colorado River still grinding away at the cut it's been making for millions of years.

Sunrise From Yavapai Point

Canyon Treefrog

Mule Ride—North Kaibab Trail

Where is Grand Canyon National Park?

Grand Canyon National Park is in the northwest part of Arizona. You can go there by car, bus, or plane. Airplanes land at Flagstaff, Arizona, or at the South Rim of Grand Canyon.

Two parts of the park are waiting for you. Many people drive to the South Rim from Flagstaff or Cameron. You can get to the higher North Rim on U.S. Highway 89 from Page to Jacob Lake. Arizona Route 67 takes you the rest of the way.

The park is open all year, but snow closes the North Rim from about mid-October to mid-May.

Two or three days at the South Rim will give you time to see most of it. But if you want to hike a lot or take a mule trip, you'll need more time.

For hiking you need loose clothing with long sleeves, a sun hat, and a water bottle or canteen. Your feet will be glad if you take strong, comfortable shoes or boots. In summer, you can rent backpacking equipment at the park or bring your own.

Find out about hotels and campgrounds by writing to the Superintendent, P.O. Box 129, Grand Canyon National Park, Grand Canyon, Arizona 86023.

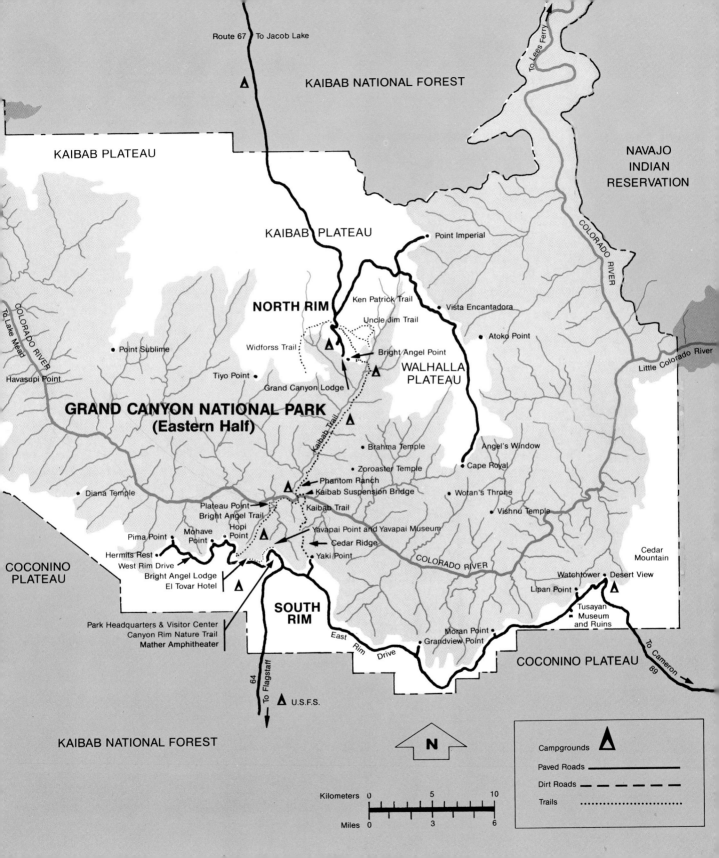

Route 67 To Jacob Lake

KAIBAB NATIONAL FOREST

KAIBAB PLATEAU

NAVAJO
INDIAN
RESERVATION

KAIBAB PLATEAU

COLORADO RIVER

To Lees Ferry

To Lake Mead

COLORADO RIVER

Point Imperial

NORTH RIM

Ken Patrick Trail
Uncle Jim Trail

Vista Encantadora

Atoko Point

Point Sublime

Widforss Trail

Bright Angel Point

WALHALLA
PLATEAU

Little Colorado River

Tiyo Point

Grand Canyon Lodge

Havasupi Point

GRAND CANYON NATIONAL PARK
(Eastern Half)

Kaibab Trail

Brahma Temple

Angel's Window

Zoroaster Temple

Cape Royal

Diana Temple

Phantom Ranch
Kaibab Suspension Bridge

Wotan's Throne

Plateau Point
Bright Angel Trail

Kaibab Trail

Vishnu Temple

Pima Point

Mohave
Point

Hopi
Point

Yavapai Point and Yavapai Museum

Cedar
Mountain

Hermits Rest

Cedar Ridge

COLORADO RIVER

West Rim Drive

Yaki Point

Watchtower • Desert View

Bright Angel Lodge
El Tovar Hotel

COCONINO
PLATEAU

Lipan Point

Tusayan Museum
and Ruins

Park Headquarters & Visitor Center
Canyon Rim Nature Trail
Mather Amphitheater

SOUTH
RIM

East Rim Drive

Moran Point

Grandview Point

COCONINO PLATEAU

To Cameron
89

64
To Flagstaff

U.S.F.S.

KAIBAB NATIONAL FOREST

N

Campgrounds	▲
Paved Roads	———
Dirt Roads	– – –
Trails	·········

Kilometers 0   5   10

Miles 0   3   6

Indian Stories

Five different Indian tribes of this area have stories or legends about the canyon and the river.

The Hopi Indians believe all living things come out of the underworld through a hole called the sipapu. After death they return to the earth the same way. To the Hopi, the sipapu is in the canyon near the meeting place of the Colorado and Little Colorado Rivers.

A Navajo story of the canyon tells how all the people turned into fish to keep from drowning in a flood. The Hualapai legend says a hero made a slash in the ground to drain flood waters from the land. Ute Indians say a god created the river to hide a trail that led to the Land of Joy.

The Havasupai, who still live in the canyon, tell of a good god and a bad one. The bad god wanted to make trouble for people, so he tried to drown the world. One Indian girl was saved by the good god who put her in a boat carved from a pinyon tree. She became the mother of the Havasupai Indians. Later, when the flood waters ran off to the sea, they cut the deep, deep "Chic a mi mi," the Grand Canyon.

Does The River Hide A Trail To The Land Of Joy? ➤

How It Came to Be

There are many ideas, or theories, about how Grand Canyon was formed. It was cut by running water. But since the Grand Canyon is cut through a raised area called a plateau, how did the water get up there to cut down and make a canyon?

One idea is that the Colorado River was in place before the land rose up in a kind of hill now called the Kaibab Plateau. The plateau rose very slowly, and as it rose, the river cut down across the hill.

Another idea is that this hill was buried under layers of rock. The river cut through those layers into the Kaibab Plateau. The upper layers of rock were later washed away.

The third theory is that one river to the west cut a deep canyon across the plateau and "captured" the flow of the Colorado River from the east.

The newest idea is that the river made its way from east to west before the land rose. Another uplift dammed the river for a while, and the river made a lake to the east. As the lake filled with mud and sand, its level rose until it overflowed into a valley and cut the Grand Canyon.

Which theory seems right to you? Maybe some day you will think of a new theory.

The Canyon Was Cut By Running Water ➤

A Story in Its Walls

As the river cut this deep canyon, it "opened a book" that tells some of the earth's history.

Geologists believe the earth is over four billion years old. The walls of the canyon show layers of rock formed during the last two billion years. The rocks near the river were once part of a mountain range as high as the highest mountains of today. But over tens of millions of years, erosion wore the range down to make a flat plain.

Water flowed across the plain and sand, or sediment, collected under a shallow sea. Sometimes the sea dried, and sediments hardened. Then a new sea formed and more sediment collected in the sea bottom. Layer upon layer formed over a very long time until they were over 4000 meters deep.

Then new earth forces tilted the rocks to form new mountains: again they were eroded away. At one time, desert sand covered this area with dunes that later changed into stone. This layering and erosion went on and on. Then some time between five and 25 million years ago, a river began to cut the Grand Canyon.

Two-Billion-Year-Old Vishnu Formation

Layer Upon Layer—Freya Castle

A Canyon Full Of Layers

The Fossil Story

About 500 million years ago, shallow seas were full of trilobites, tiny sea animals. When they died, some trilobites were buried in wet sand under the water. Minerals in the water replaced the cells of their bodies. As thousands and millions of years passed, some of these trilobites petrified. The petrified trilobites were fossils, ancient forms of life turned to stone. A fossil can also be an animal's footprint or the print of a leaf or an insect wing.

There are no fossils at the bottom of the canyon. About 1.7 billion years ago all traces of life were destroyed when those rocks metamorphosed. They changed from one kind of a rock to another. Rock layers higher in the canyon hold fossils of trilobites. Near the rim, where rocks are more than 200 million years old, are fossils of modern life forms like seashells and reptile footprints.

You can see a fossil collection at the Yavapai Museum. If you are lucky enough to find a fossil, look at it. Imagine how long it's been here. You can even take its picture. But leave it for others to see, because the fossils in Grand Canyon belong to everyone.

Trilobite In Bright Angel Shale

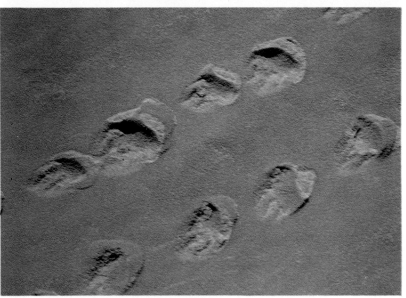

Reptile Footprints In Coconino Sandstone

Gastropod In Kaibab Limestone

Insect Wing In Hermit Shale

Grand Canyon Hiking

Grand Canyon hiking is different from almost any other hiking because of the hot, dry climate. On a hike into the canyon and out again, the hardest part of the hike comes at the end when you're tired.

Park Rangers say you need about two liters of water per person per day going down into the canyon in summer. Going back up takes twice as much water as going down. You need less water in winter, but beware of freezing cold, rain, sleet, and snow.

Rangers warn against bare skin. They say to wear a thin layer of light-colored clothes and a light hat. In summer it gets as hot as 40° Celsius at the bottom of the canyon. So you should hike in the coolest part of the day and rest in shade during midday.

You don't need a permit to day-hike. But if you plan to camp overnight, you need a permit and a reservation for a campsite. For these, it's best to write early to Backcountry Reservations Office, Grand Canyon National Park, Grand Canyon, Arizona 86023.

Boy Scouts Hike Up North Kaibab Trail

You May See Lizards—Collared Lizard

South Rim Trails

For shorter hikes, the South Rim has good trails. Self-guiding leaflets help you understand what you see along the Canyon Rim Nature Trail from El Tovar Hotel to the Visitor Center. More of the trail goes from there to the Yavapai Museum. At this point you can see way down to the Vishnu Formation near the river. Rangers on duty explain canyon formations and give programs.

Toward the west, a trail goes along the edge of the canyon from Bright Angel Lodge. You can take a short walk on this trail or go almost 13 kilometers to Hermits Rest.

You can also take shorter hikes down the inner canyon trails from South Rim. A good half-day hike is down the Kaibab Trail from Yaki Point to Cedar Ridge. You must carry your own water, about one liter per person.

Bright Angel Trail was first made by animals, then used by people. A hike partway down this trail should be measured in time, not distance. If you hike down for one hour, it will take two hours or more to hike back up. Take water, and remember, going back means going up, always a bit harder.

View Of Bright Angel Trail From West Rim

Day-Hikers—South Kaibab Trail

Old Dan Canyon

As you hike, you may think about the Grand Canyon tales you've heard. Some are true, some not so true. There are tales about the Last Chance and Orphan Mines, horse thieves, and hidden gold.

A modern young man who works here every summer tells tales of Old Dan Canyon. Dan's the one who paints the Red Wall and spreads a purple haze in the air at sunset. He has a special polish to shine up the stars in a black night sky.

Old Dan Canyon is the hiker who passes you with a quick, light step when you're trudging and puffing up the trail. He doesn't even sweat!

Dan has a list of hiking tips for you to remember. ''1. From river to rim, through your lungs and your skin, you lose eight liters of water. 2. You can't fail if you stay on the trail. 3. Trash left in the canyon will litter your dreams. 4. The canyon is home for lizards and snakes, so please do not disturb. 5. If you think you see me, OK. If you think you hear me talking, you're in trouble. You've been in the sun too long without a hat.''

Dan Paints The Red Wall—

And Spreads A Purple Haze

The North Rim

If you were Dan Canyon, you could cross the canyon on a bolt of lightning. An eagle or raven can fly the 16-kilometer hop from South to North Rim. Strong hikers walk from rim to rim in two days with an overnight stay at Phantom Ranch. Others may spend four days and take time to see more.

The drive from South Rim to North Rim on good roads takes about six hours. Once there, you'll see the beautiful old Grand Canyon Lodge. It almost hangs over the canyon. Nearby, a short trail takes you to Bright Angel Point. It's the place to be when the canyon changes colors at sunset and sunrise.

If you walk quietly on the Uncle Jim or Ken Patrick Trails, you'll see birds and squirrels hunting for food.

While at North Rim, you can drive or take a tour bus to Point Imperial and Cape Royal. You can stop at points along the way to get different views of the canyon. Just before Cape Royal is where you see Angel's Window. Then at Cape Royal you look across one of the widest parts of the canyon. From here you can see Wotan's Throne and Vishnu Temple.

Raven

From Bright Angel Point At Sunset—Brahma And Zoroaster Temples

Angel's Window

Vishnu Temple From Cape Royal

How's the Weather?

Grand Canyon has many different elevations and different kinds of weather, or climate.

Deep in the canyon, it's very hot in the summer and dry. Desert plants and animals like cacti and snakes live there.

High on the North Rim, it's more like the mountains. Deer and squirrels live among pine, fir, and aspen trees.

At a lower elevation, the South Rim has a mixture of high desert and mountain climates. It snows in winter, and you find squirrels, chipmunks, and deer. Pinyon pines and junipers shelter agave, Mormon tea, and some wild flowers.

Between the canyon rims and the river are other kinds of climates. Slopes facing south are dried by the sun. Canyon walls and edges are dried by hot air rising from the desert below. At low places along the rim, cooler, heavier air spills into the canyon.

A hike into the canyon takes you through different climates, and you see different kinds of plants and animals.

Many Elevations—Many Climates—From Widforss Trail, North Rim

Sometimes It's Cold

Both plants and animals live where the weather is right for them. At the North Rim where it snows in winter, you find trees like Douglas-fir, white fir, and Engelmann spruce. Their thin evergreen needles can stand more cold than trees with flat, wide leaves. The aspen tree loses its wide leaves in the fall, so its bare branches don't hold snow that could break them.

Trees and other plants of the North Rim give food and shelter to many animals. Most of them have furry coats that keep them warm. Small animals crawl into underground homes to get away from cold. Some hibernate, or go into a very deep sleep. When they hibernate, they don't burn up as much energy, and they live on fat stored up during the summer.

Some of the bigger animals of the canyon—ringtail cat, cougar, and mule deer—can move from one type of climate to another. There are some deer on the South Rim and more on the North Rim. You may even see deer at Indian Gardens and Phantom Ranch in the Inner Canyon desert.

Aspen With Spruce And Fir

Mule Deer

The Tassel-eared Squirrel

During the Ice Age, much of North America was covered with snow and ice. When the ice melted about 10,000 years ago, the canyon was wet and cool. Ponderosa pines grew at lower elevations in the canyon. A squirrel with bushy ears, the tassel-eared squirrel, lived in these trees and ate their seeds and twigs.

Then the region dried out. Ponderosas died in the lower, hot desert areas, but continued to grov in cooler places along canyon rims. The canyon's desert separated the squirrels of the South Rim from those on the North Rim. During the past thousands of years, they have changed into two different kinds, or subspecies, of tassel-eared squirrels.

Now the Abert squirrel lives on the South Rim and in other places of the U.S. and Mexico. Another tassel-eared squirrel, the Kaibab, lives only on the north side of the canyon. Both of them have gray bodies. But the Kaibab has a black belly and bushy white tail, while most Aberts have white bellies and gray tails.

This squirrel is shy and quiet. You must look carefully to see a Kaibab squirrel high in the ponderosa pines of the North Rim and the nearby Kaibab National Forest.

Aspen And Ponderosa

Look Quickly! It's A Rare Kaibab Squirrel!

Kaibab Squirrel In Ponderosa Pine

Between Rims and River

It's drier below the rims where plants like Gambel oak and Utah juniper grow. A juniper's leaves are tiny scales that give off very little water. It grows slowly but can live more than 2000 years.

Prickly plants like Yucca and cactus have special skins that hold moisture.

Lizards and snakes live in these drier areas of Grand Canyon, and some live on the rims. The short-horned lizard lives in the pine and fir forest as well as among pinyon, juniper, and desert plants. This lizard is hard to find because its skin color helps it hide. It can also bury itself in the sand while a skin flap keeps sand from getting in its nose.

You may find a short-horned lizard in a rotting log where it hunts ants to eat. Or you may find it trying to soak up more sun by flattening itself against a rock.

If the horned lizard sees you, it may puff up in fear. It may even burst the little sacks in its eyes, causing blood to squirt at you.

Is a lizard afraid of a snake? Maybe, but the snake should be more afraid to swallow a lizard all covered with horns.

Gambel Oak Leaves In Fall

Utah Juniper

Horned Lizard

Sometimes It's Hot

A raindrop can dry out, or evaporate, before it reaches the bottom of the canyon. But prickly pear and other cacti make the most of a yearly rainfall of only about 20 centimeters. Shallow roots reach out to gather water from a wide area. Thick, waxy skins keep water from evaporating from the plant.

Snakes do not sweat, so they don't lose much water through their scaly skins. A reptile's blood stays at almost the same temperature as the air around it. If the air is too cold, a snake slows its heartbeat and breathing while it hibernates in a warm place. When the air is too hot, it gets very still and estivates, or goes into a deep sleep.

Two kinds, or subspecies, of the western rattlesnake live in the canyon: the Great Basin and the pink Grand Canyon rattler. Other rattlesnakes in the canyon are the speckled and black-tailed. Many snakes want to hide or get away from people. But watch out for the more dangerous black-tailed rattlesnake. It may fight or attack.

Careful hikers know they should wear leg covering and heavy boots. They stay away from rock piles, shrubs, and cracks or holes where snakes may be resting.

Prickly Pear, One Of Many Kinds of Cacti

Great Basin Rattlesnake

Getting Around the Park

With so many interesting things to see and do, you may wonder how you'll get around. You can drive on both rims in a car, park, and get out to see many different canyon views. On East Rim Drive of the South Rim, you can stop at Desert View, Moran, Lipan, and other Points to gaze into the canyon.

Once in the South Rim Grand Canyon Village, you can park your car and forget it. In spring and summer, a free Canyon Shuttle bus will take you almost anywhere: Yavapai Museum, the Visitor Center, any hotel.

All summer near Bright Angel Hotel, the Village Shuttle connects with the West Rim Shuttle. Since no cars are allowed on West Rim Drive in summer, this is a good way to see Hopi and other Points on this road. The sunrise and sunset specials are favorite rides on the West Rim.

In summer, you can rent a bicycle at Maricopa Point. This is a fairly safe place to ride, but watch out for the shuttle bus. (Get your bicycle before the rush.)

Between the free Canyon Shuttle, bicycles, and your own two feet, you can see a lot of Grand Canyon National Park.

Canyon Shuttle And Your Own Two Feet

Bicycle On West Rim

Your Long-eared Friend

You can also get around Grand Canyon on your friend, the mule. You can go on an all-day trip from the South Rim down Bright Angel Trail to Plateau Point.

The two-day Phantom Ranch Trip goes on all year. From the South Rim, you go to the end of Bright Angel Trail. As you ride by the river, you'll hear why the Havasu Indians called this "The Place of Roaring Sound." Then your mule takes you along the River Trail, through a tunnel, and across the Kaibab Suspension Bridge. After riding awhile on the north section of the Kaibab Trail, mule riders gladly get off their long-eared "taxis" and relax at the Phantom Ranch. A dip in the cold waters of Bright Angel Creek washes away some of the "ouch." Then dinner, sleep, and very early breakfast put everyone back in shape to ride up the South Kaibab Trail to Yaki Point.

If you are at least 12 years old and weigh less than 91 kilograms, you can buy a South Rim mule trip from Fred Harvey Reservations, Grand Canyon, Arizona 86023. Write the North Rim Ranger Station, North Rim, Arizona 86022, to find out about mule trips from there.

Long-Eared Taxis Take You Down The Canyon—

And Back Up

To Cross the River

Three bridges cross the river in Grand Canyon: the Navajo Bridge for vehicles near Lees Ferry and two suspension bridges near Phantom Ranch.

Until 1907, the only way to cross the river was by some kind of ferry or boat. In the 1900s, E.D. Woolley formed a company to make a trail from the North to the South Rim. Men of this company built a hanging cable car across the river. It had a wooden cage big enough for a man and a mule. In 1921 they built a swinging bridge.

The Kaibab Suspension Bridge in use today was built in 1928. This stronger, safer bridge is 134 meters long and about 24 meters above low water. To make this bridge, workers carried many tons of steel down the Kaibab Trail from Yaki Point. The bridge is made of eight cables, each thicker than a garden hose and 167 meters long. It took forty-two Havasupai Indians to carry each unrolled cable down the trail. They stood three or four meters apart, lifted the cable, and started down the trail, snaking around the curves into the canyon.

The bridge they built is strong enough to hold many hikers and mules at one time.

Kaibab Suspension Bridge

River Trips

Each year millions of people gaze down into the canyon from the rims. Those who hike or ride a mule to the river get to see the canyon from the bottom. If you save enough money, you can see the canyon from a raft or boat on the river.

Several companies operate different kinds of river trips. It takes about two weeks to go on the longest river trip from Lees Ferry to Lake Mead. It also takes a strong hold on the boat and a bit of courage until you get used to the river. Inflated rafts called baloney boats take people over river rapids. At times waves cover the raft from both sides. You may find yourself sitting in water while you bail out the raft with a bucket. But your clothes dry in the hot desert air before you even think of changing them. Your guide says the raft won't tip over, but you're not sure if you can believe it.

Write to the Superintendent at Grand Canyon National Park, Grand Canyon, Arizona 86023, for names of companies that operate river trips.

A Quiet Time On The River

A River Trip Is Pure Adventure

The Rangers

At both rims, Park Rangers have many stories to tell you. North and South Rim Rangers take young people on nature walks. They tell about plants and animals of the park. Every evening from June 15 to Labor Day, a North Rim Ranger shows slides in the Grand Canyon Lodge.

On East Rim Drive of the South Rim, a Ranger takes visitors around the Tusayan Ruins. Visitors can think their way back to the 12th century when about 30 people lived in stone houses on this spot. In the museum nearby, you can see the baskets they wove and the clay pots they made.

Also at the South Rim, you can join a nature walk. Starting at the Visitor Center, you walk with a Ranger to Yavapai Point. You stop at different places to learn about plants like the agave, a plant that takes many years to bloom. The agave plant dies as it blooms and goes to seed.

Evenings, Rangers show slides at the Mather Amphitheater behind the South Rim Visitor Center.

All of these programs change from season to season and year to year. The free park newspaper will tell you when and where Rangers guide walks and give talks.

Ranger Explains Tusayan Ruins—East Rim Drive

Agave Plant

Agave Bloom

A Story Without an Ending?

Is your story of Grand Canyon complete? Do you know how the early people lived? Who first dared to ride down the river? How will the story end? Is it true the canyon may be a flat plain ten million years from now? Answers to these and many other questions are in the interesting exhibits at the Visitor Center and the Tusayan and Yavapai Museums.

Now you need "picture memories" to go with your stories. Some say it takes time to find the best way to *see* the canyon. You can begin at sunrise or sunset by sitting at your favorite spot on the rim. Be quiet and feel the wind on your face. Let your hands move over the ripply rocks beside you. Listen to the ravens. Smell the fresh clean air around you.

Look at one part of the canyon with its rocky ridges. See the smooth sandy plateaus dotted with plants. Watch the colors change. Each time you look at a different part, you find a whole new canyon, a whole new story.

After your last look, close your eyes and promise yourself to remember the stories of Grand Canyon National Park.

Everyone Has A Special Way To See Grand Canyon

Zoroaster Temple

Another Park in Arizona

PETRIFIED FOREST NATIONAL PARK lies within the Painted Desert of northern Arizona. In it are the remains of fallen trees that have turned to stone.

The trees petrified in a process that took millions of years. Many years ago, trees fell into streams where they were buried in mud, sand, and volcanic ash. Slowly, the grain of the trees filled with water rich in a mineral called silica, or quartz. Bit by bit, the silica replaced the wood cells of the tree. The tree changed from wood to rock.

The rising of earth layers allowed erosion to uncover the petrified logs. Now they lie on the surface, fantastic works of natural art.

Many hiking trails lead to the most beautiful areas with petrified wood. You may feel like taking some petrified wood home. But it's against the law to take even the smallest piece. Isn't it better to leave the petrified wood where nature left it? Then future visitors can enjoy the wonders that took millions of years to create.

Petrified Forest National Park

Petrified Wood

The Author and Illustrator

Wyoming-born Ruth Radlauer's love for national parks began with Yellowstone. In her younger years she spent her summers in the Bighorn Mountains, at Yellowstone, or in the mountains near Casper.

Ed and Ruth Radlauer, graduates of the University of California at Los Angeles, are authors of many books for young people. Their subjects range from social studies to youth activities such as horse riding and motorcycling.

The Radlauers live in California, where they spend most of their time in the mountains near Los Angeles.

Photographing the national parks is a labor of love for Rolf Zillmer and his wife Evelyn. Because they are backpackers and wildlife enthusiasts, the Zillmers can give a truly intimate view of each park.

A former student at Art Center College of Design in Los Angeles, Mr. Zillmer was born in New York City. He now makes his home in Los Angeles, California, where he does painting, sculpture, and most of the art direction for Elk Grove Books.